From Larry & Lisa,

Mothers Day.

1983

Poems of Sentiment & Inspiration

Poems of Sentiment & Inspiration

COMPILED BY MARY SANFORD LAURENCE

A HART BOOK

A & W PUBLISHERS • NEW YORK

PUBLISHED BY
A & W PUBLISHERS, INC.
95 MADISON AVENUE
NEW YORK, NEW YORK 10016

LIBRARY OF CONGRESS CATALOG CARD NO. 81-66208

ISBN: 0-89479-090-0

PRINTED IN THE UNITED STATES OF AMERICA

Contents

COURAGE

FACING DEATH

FAITH

FRIENDSHIP

MOTHER

PATRIOTISM

PHILOSOPHY

REMEMBRANCE

REVERENCE FOR LIFE

ROMANCE

THOUGHTFULNESS

Poems of Sentiment & Inspiration

Foreword

Poetry can express the familiar, and the unfamiliar; the ordinary and the extraordinary. Matthew Arnold said, "Poetry is simply the most beautiful, impressive, and widely effective mode of saying things. And the things poets say can be as simple as a smile, or as deep as pain."

With economy of words and beauty of words, the poet strikes the exact note to which you resound. Coleridge put the art of the poet very simply when he said that "prose consists of words in their best order, but poetry consists of the best words in their best order."

The poems in this book were selected because they are the kinds of poems you will want to remember, the kind you will want to read again and again. These poems celebrate friendship, faith, home, patriotism, and love; they deal with courage, compassion, fear, grief. In other words, here are poems for every occasion, whether joyous or sad. Here, also, is homespun, common-sense truth, as well as profound revelation.

POEMS OF SENTIMENT AND INSPIRATION is a book you will cherish. It is sure to become one of your personal treasures.

BROTHERHOOD

Outwitted

He drew a circle that shut me out—
Heretic, rebel, a thing to flout.
But Love and I had the wit to win:
We drew a circle that took him in!

EDWIN MARKHAM

Who Are My People?

My people? Who are they?
I went into the church where the congregation
Worshipped my God. Were they my people?
I felt no kinship to them as they knelt there.
My people! Where are they?
I went into the land where I was born,
Where men spoke my language. . .
I was a stranger there.
"My people," my soul cried. "Who are my people?"

Last night in the rain I met an old man
Who spoke a language I do not speak,
Which marked him as one who does not
        know my God.
With apologetic smile he offered me
The shelter of his patched umbrella.
I met his eyes . . . And then I knew. . . .

ROSA ZAGNONI MARINONI

A Thing of Beauty

A thing of beauty is a joy for ever:
Its loveliness increases; it will never
Pass into nothingness; but still will keep
A bower quiet for us, and a sleep
Full of sweet dreams, and health, and quiet breathing.
Therefore, on every morrow, are we wreathing
A flowery band to bind us to the earth,
Spite of despondence, of the inhuman dearth
Of noble natures, of the gloomy days,
Of all the unhealthy and o'er-darkened ways
Made for our searching: yes, in spite of all,
Some shape of beauty moves away the pall
From our dark spirits.

JOHN KEATS

Leisure

What is this life if, full of care,
We have no time to stand and stare.

No time to stand beneath the boughs
And stare as long as sheep or cows.

No time to see, when woods we pass,
Where squirrels hide their nuts in grass.

No time to see, in broad daylight,
Streams full of stars, like skies at night.

No time to turn at Beauty's glance,
And watch her feet, how they can dance.

No time to wait till her mouth can
Enrich that smile her eyes began.

A poor life this if, full of care,
We have no time to stand and stare.

WILLIAM HENRY DAVIES

Sea-Fever

I must go down to the seas again, to the lonely sea
and the sky,
And all I ask is a tall ship and a star to steer her by,
And the wheel's kick and the wind's song and the
white sail's shaking,
And a gray mist on the sea's face and a gray dawn
breaking.

I must go down to the seas again, for the call of the
running tide
Is a wild call and a clear call that may not be denied;
And all I ask is a windy day with the white clouds
flying,
And the flung spray and the blown spume, and the
sea-gulls crying.

I must go down to the seas again to the vagrant gypsy
life.
To the gull's way and the whale's way where the
wind's like a whetted knife;
And all I ask is a merry yarn from a laughing fellow-
rover,
And quiet sleep and a sweet dream when the long
trick's over.

JOHN MASEFIELD

There Is No Death

There is no death! The stars go down
   To rise upon some other shore,
And bright in heaven's jeweled crown
   They shine for evermore.

There is no death! The dust we tread
   Shall change beneath the summer showers
To golden grain or mellow fruit
   Or rainbow-tinted flowers.

There is no death! The leaves may fall,
   The flowers may fade and pass away—
They only wait, through wintry hours,
   The coming of the May.

The bird-like voice, whose joyous tones
   Made glad this scene of sin and strife,
Sings now an everlasting song
   Amid the tree of life.

And ever near us, though unseen,
   The dear immortal spirits tread;
For all the boundless universe
   Is Life—there are no dead!

JOHN LUCKEY MCCREERY

CHILDHOOD

Making A Man

Hurry the baby as fast as you can,
Hurry him, worry him, make him a man.
Off with his baby clothes, get him in pants,
Feed him on brain foods and make him advance.
Hustle him, soon as he's able to walk,
Into a grammar school; cram him with talk.
Fill his poor head full of figures and facts,
Keep on a-jamming them in till it cracks.
Once boys grew up at a rational rate,
Now we develop a man while you wait,
Rush him through college, compel him to grab,
Of every known subject a dip and a dab.
Get him in business and after the cash,
All by the time he can grow a mustache
Let him forget he was ever a boy,
Make gold his god and its jingle his joy.
Keep him a-hustling and clear out of breath,
Until he wins—nervous prostration and death.

NIXON WATERMAN

Where Did You Come From?

Where did you come from, Baby dear?
Out of the everywhere into here.

Where did get your eyes so blue?
Out of the sky as I came through.

What makes the light in them sparkle and spin?
Some of the starry spikes left in.

Where did you get that little tear?
I found it waiting when I got here.

What makes your forehead so smooth and high?
A soft hand stroked it as I went by.

What makes your cheek like a warm white rose?
I saw something better than anyone knows.

Whence that three-corner'd smile of bliss?
Three angels gave me at once a kiss.

Where did you get this pearly ear?
God spoke, and it came out to hear.

Where did you get those arms and hands?
Love made itself into hooks and bands.

Feet, whence did you come, you darling things?
From the same box as the cherubs' wings.

How did they all come just to be you?
God thought of me, and so I grew.

But how did you come to us, you dear?
God thought of you, and so I am here.

GEORGE MACDONALD

COMPASSION

Charity

There is so much good in the worst of us,
And so much bad in the best of us,
That it ill behooves any of us
To find fault with the rest of us.

UNKNOWN

Fleurette

My leg? It's off at the knee.
Do I miss it? Well, some. You see
I've had it since I was born;
And lately a devilish corn.
(I rather chuckle with glee
To think how I've fooled that corn.)

But I'll hobble around all right.
It isn't that, it's my face.
Oh I know I'm a hideous sight,
Hardly a thing in place;
Sort of gargoyle, you'd say.
Nurse won't give me a glass,
But I see the folks as they pass
Shudder and turn away;
Turn away in distress. . .
Mirror enough, I guess.

I'm gay! You bet I *am* gay;
But I wasn't a while ago.
If you'd seen me even to-day,
The darndest picture of woe,
With this Caliban mug of mine,
So ravaged and raw and red,
Turned to the wall—in fine,
Wishing that I was dead. . . .

So over the blanket's rim
I raised my terrible face,
And I saw—how I envied him!
A girl of such delicate grace;
Sixteen, all laughter and love;
As gay as a linnet, and yet
As tenderly sweet as a dove;
Half woman, half child—Fleurette.

What has happened since then,
Since I lay with my face to the wall,
The most despairing of men?
Listen! I'll tell you all.

That *poilu* across the way,
With the shrapnel wound in his head,
Has a sister: she came to-day
To sit awhile by his bed.
All morning I heard him fret:
"Oh, when will she come, Fleurette?"

Then sudden, a joyous cry;
The tripping of little feet;
The softest, tenderest sigh;
A voice so fresh and sweet;
Clear as a silver bell,
Fresh as the morning dews:
"C'est toi, c'est toi, Marcel!
Mon frère, comme je suis heureuse!"

Then I turned to the wall again.
(I was awfully blue, you see,)
And I thought with a bitter pain:
"Such visions are not for me."

So there like a log I lay,
All hidden, I thought, from view,
When sudden I heard her say:
"Ah! Who is that *malheureux?*"
Then briefly I heard him tell
(However he came to know)
How I'd smothered a bomb that fell
Into the trench, and so
None of my men were hit,
Though it busted me up a bit.

Well, I didn't quiver an eye,
And he chattered and there she sat;
And I fancied I heard her sigh—
But I wouldn't just swear to that.
And maybe she wasn't so bright,
Though she talked in a merry strain,
And I closed my eyes ever so tight,
Yet I saw her ever so plain:
Her dear little tilted nose,
Her delicate, dimpled chin,
Her mouth like a budding rose,
And the glistening pearls within;
Her eyes like the violet:
Such a rare little queen—Fleurette.

And at last when she rose to go,
The light was a little dim,
And I ventured to peep, and so
I saw her, graceful and slim,
And she kissed him and kissed him, and oh
How I envied and envied him!

So when she was gone I said
In rather a dreary voice
To him of the opposite bed:
"Ah, friend, how you must rejoice!
But me, I'm a thing of dread.
For me nevermore the bliss,
The thrill of a woman's kiss."

Then I stopped, for lo! she was there,
And a great light shone in her eyes.
And me! I could only stare,
I was taken so by surprise,
When gently she bent her head:
"May I kiss you, Sergeant?" she said.

Then she kissed my burning lips
With her mouth like a scented flower,
And I thrilled to the finger-tips,
And I hadn't even the power
To say: "God bless you, dear!"
And I felt such a precious tear
Fall on my withered cheek,
And darn it! I couldn't speak.
And so she went sadly away,
And I knew that my eyes were wet.
Ah, not to my dying day
Will I forget, forget!
Can you wonder now I am gay?
God bless her, that little Fleurette!

ROBERT SERVICE

COURAGE

Curfew Must Not Ring Tonight

Slowly England's sun was setting o'er the hilltops far
away,
Filling all the land with beauty at the close of one sad
day;
And the last rays kissed the forehead of a man and a
maiden fair,
He with footsteps slow and weary, she with sunny
floating hair;
He with bowed head, sad and thoughtful, she with
lips all cold and white,
Struggling to keep back the murmur, "Curfew must
not ring tonight!"

"Sexton," Bessie's white lips faltered, pointing to the
      prison old,
With its turrets tall and gloomy, with its walls, dark,
      damp and cold—
"I've a lover in the prison, doomed this very night to
      die
At the ringing of the curfew, and no earthly help is
      nigh!
Cromwell will not come till sunset"; and her face
      grew strangely white
As she breathed the husky whisper, "Curfew must not
      ring tonight!"

"Bessie," calmly spoke the sexton—and his accents
      pierced her heart
Like the piercing of an arrow, like a deadly poisoned
      dart—
"Long, long years I've rung the curfew from that
      gloomy, shadowed tower;
Every evening, just at sunset, it has told the twilight
      hour;
I have done my duty ever, tried to do it just and
      right—
Now I'm old I still must do it: Curfew, girl, must ring
      tonight!"

Wild her eyes and pale her features, stern and white
     her thoughtful brow,
And within her secret bosom Bessie made a solemn
     vow.
She had listened while the judges read, without a tear
     or sigh,
"At the ringing of the curfew, Basil Underwood must
     die."
And her breath came fast and faster, and her eyes grew
     large and bright,
As in undertone she murmured, "Curfew must not
     ring tonight!"

With quick step she bounded forward, sprang within
     the old church door,
Left the old man threading slowly paths he'd often
     trod before;
Not one moment paused the maiden, but with eye and
     cheek aglow
Mounted up the gloomy tower, where the bell swung
     to and fro
As she climbed the dusty ladder, on which fell no ray
     of light,
Up and up, her white lips saying, "Curfew shall not
     ring tonight!"

She has reached the topmost ladder, o'er her hangs
      the great dark bell:
Awful is the gloom beneath her, like the pathway
      down to hell!
Lo, the ponderous tongue is swinging.
      'Tis the hour of curfew now,
And the sight has chilled her bosom, stopped her
      breath and paled her brow;
Shall she let it ring? No, never! Flash her eyes with
      sudden light,
And she springs and grasps it firmly:
      "Curfew shall not ring tonight!"

Out she swung, far out; the city seemed a speck of
      light below;
She 'twixt heaven and earth suspended as the bell
      swung to and fro;
And the sexton at the bell rope, old and deaf, heard
      not the bell,
But he thought it still was ringing fair young Basil's
      funeral knell.
Still the maiden clung more firmly, and, with trem-
      bling lips and white,
Said, to hush her heart's wild beating, "Curfew shall
      not ring tonight!"

It was o'er; the bell ceased swaying, and the maiden
    stepped once more
Firmly on the dark old ladder, where for hundred
    years before
Human foot had not been planted; but the brave deed
    she had done
Should be told long ages after—often as the setting
    sun
Should illume the sky with beauty, aged sires, with
    heads of white,
Long should tell the little children, "Curfew did not
    ring that night."

O'er the distant hills came Cromwell; Bessie sees him,
    and her brow,
Full of hope and full of gladness, has no anxious
    traces now.
At his feet she tells her story, shows her hands all
    bruised and torn;
And her face so sweet and pleading, yet with sorrow
    pale and worn,
Touched his heart with sudden pity—lit his eye with
    misty light;
"Go, your lover lives!" said Cromwell; "Curfew shall
    not ring tonight!"

Wide they flung the massive portals, led the prisoner
      forth to die,
All his bright young life before him. 'Neath the
      darkening English sky
Bessie came with flying footsteps, eyes aglow with
      love-light sweet;
Kneeling on the turf beside him, laid a pardon at his
      feet.
In his brave, strong arms he clasped her, kissed the
      face upturned and white,
Whispered, "Darling, you have saved me; curfew will
      not ring tonight."

ROSE HARTWICK THORPE

The Hell-Gate of Soissons

My name is Darino, the poet. You have heard? *Oui,*
    Comédie Française.
Perchance it has happened, *mon ami,* you know of
    my unworthy lays.
Ah, then you must guess how my fingers are itching
    to talk to a pen;
For I was at Soissons, and saw it, the death of the
    twelve Englishmen.

My leg, *malheureusement,* I left it behind on the
    banks of the Aisne.
Regret? I would pay with the other to witness their
    valor again.
A trifle, indeed, I assure you, to give for the honor to
    tell
How that handful of British, undaunted, went into the
    Gateway of Hell.

Let me draw you a plan of the battle. Here we French
    and your Engineers stood;
Over there a detachment of German sharpshooters lay
    hid in a wood.
A *mitrailleuse* battery planted on top of this well-
    chosen ridge
Held the road for the Prussians and covered the direct
    approach to the bridge.

It was madness to dare the dense murder that spewed
    from those ghastly machines.
(Only those who have danced to its music can know
    what the *mitrailleuse* means.)
But the bridge on the Aisne was a menace; our safety
    demanded its fall:
"Engineers—volunteers!" In a body, the Royals stood
    out at the call.

Death at best was the fate of that mission—to their
    glory not one was dismayed.
A party was chosen—and seven survived till the
    powder was laid.
And *they* died with their fuses unlighted. Another
    detachment! Again
A sortie is made—all too vainly. The bridge still
    commanded the Aisne.

We were fighting two foes—Time and Prussia—the
    moments were worth more than troops.
We *must* blow up the bridge. A lone soldier darts out
    from the Royals and swoops
For the fuse! Fate seems with us. We cheer him; he
    answers—our hopes are reborn!
A ball rips his visor—his khaki shows red where
    another has torn.

Will he live—will he last—will he make it? *Hélas!*
    And so near to the goal!
A second, he dies! Then a third one! A fourth! Still the
    Germans take toll!
A fifth, *magnifique!* It is magic! How does he escape
    them? He may. . .
Yes, he *does!* See, the match flares! A rifle rings out
    from the wood and says "Nay!"

Six, seven, eight, nine take their places; six, seven,
    eight, nine brave their hail:
Six, seven, eight, nine—how we count them! But the
    sixth, seventh, eighth, and ninth fail!
A tenth! *Sacré nom!* But these English are soldiers—
    they know how to try;
(He fumbles the place where his jaw was)—they
    show, too, how heroes can die.

Ten we count—ten who ventured unquailing—ten
    there were—and ten are no more!
Yet another salutes and superbly essays where the ten
    failed before.
God of Battles, look down and protect him! Lord, his
    heart is as Thine—let him live!
But the *mitrailleuse* splutters and stutters, and riddles
    him into a sieve.

Then I thought of my sins, and sat waiting the charge
     that we could not withstand.
And I thought of my beautiful Paris, and gave a
     last look at the land,
At France, my *belle France,* in her glory of blue sky
     and green field and wood.
Death with honor, but never surrender. And to die
     with such men—it was good.

They are forming—the bugles are blaring—they will
     cross in a moment and then—
When out of the line of the Royals (your island, *mon
     ami,* breeds men)
Bursts a private, a tawny-haired giant—it was
     hopeless, but *ciel* how he ran!
Bon Dieu please remember the pattern, and make
     many more on his plan!

No cheers from our ranks, and the Germans, they
     halted in wonderment, too;
See, he reaches the bridge; ah! he lights it! I am
     dreaming, it *cannot* be true.
Screams of rage! *Fusillade!* They have killed him! Too
     late though, the good work is done.
By the valor of twelve English martyrs, the Hell-Gate
     of Soissons is won!

HERBERT KAUFMAN

Horatius

Lars Porsena of Clusium
    By the Nine Gods he swore
That the great house of Tarquin
    Should suffer wrong no more.
By the Nine Gods he swore it,
    And named a trysting day,
And bade his messengers ride forth,
East and west and south and north,
    To summon his array.

East and west and south and north
    The messengers ride fast,
And tower and town and cottage
    Have heard the trumpet's blast.
Shame on the false Etruscan
    Who lingers in his home
When Porsena of Clusium
    Is on the march for Rome.

And now hath every city
    Sent up her tale of men;
The foot are fourscore thousand,
    The horse are thousands ten.
Before the gates of Sutirum
    Is met the great array.
A proud man was Lars Porsena
    Upon the trysting day.

Now from the rock Tarpeian,
    Could the wan burghers spy
The line of blazing villages
    Red in the midnight sky.
The fathers of the City,
    They sat all night and day,
For every hour some horseman came
    With tidings of dismay.

I wis, in all the Senate,
    There was no heart so bold,
But sore it ached, and fast it beat,
    When that ill news was told.
Forthwith up rose the Consul,
    Up rose the Fathers all;
In haste they girded up their gowns,
    And hied them to the wall.

They held a council standing
    Before the River-gate;
Short time was there, ye well may guess,
    For musing or debate.
Out spake the Consul roundly:
    "The bridge must straight go down;
For, since Janiculum is lost,
    Naught else can save the town."

Just then a scout came flying,
    All wild with haste and fear:
"To arms! to arms! Sir Consul;
    Lars Porsena is here."
On the low hills to westward
    The Consul fixed his eye,
And saw the swarthy storm of dust
    Rise fast along the sky.

And the Consul's brow was sad,
    And the Consul's speech was low,
And darkly looked he at the wall,
    And darkly at the foe.
"Their van will be upon us
    Before the bridge goes down;
And if they once may win the bridge,
    What hope to save the town?"

Then out spake brave Horatius,
    The Captain of the gate:
"To every man upon this earth
    Death cometh soon or late.
And how can man die better
    Than facing fearful odds,
For the ashes of his fathers
    And the temples of his Gods!

"Hew down the bridge, Sir Consul,
    With all the speed ye may;
I, with two more to help me,
    Will hold the foe in play.
In yon strait path a thousand
    May well be stopped by three.
Now who will stand on either hand,
    And keep the bridge with me?"

Then out spake Spurius Lartius;
    A Ramnian proud was he:
"Lo, I will stand at thy right hand,
    And keep the bridge with thee."
And out spake strong Herminius;
    Of Titan blood was he:
"I will abide on thy left side,
    And keep the bridge with thee."

Now while the Three were tightening
    Their harness on their backs,
The Consul was the foremost man
    To take in hand an axe:
And Fathers mixed with Commons
    Seized hatchet, bar, and crow,
And smote upon the planks above,
    And loosed the props below.

The Three stood calm and silent
  And looked upon the foes,
And a great shout of laughter
  From all the vanguard rose:
And forth three chiefs came spurring
  Before that deep array;
To earth they sprang, their swords they drew,
And lifted high their shields, and flew
  To win the narrow way;

Aunus from green Tifernum,
  Lord of the Hill of Vines;
And Seius, whose eight hundred slaves
  Sicken in Ilva's mines;
And Picus, long to Clusium
  Vassal in peace and war,
Who led to fight his Umbrian powers
From that gray crag where, girt with towers,
The fortress of Nequinum lowers
  O'er the pale waves of Nar.

Stout Lartius hurled down Aunus
  Into the stream beneath:
Herminius struck at Seius,
  And clove him to the teeth:

At Picus brave Horatius
    Darted one fiery thrust;
And the proud Umbrian's gilded arms
    Clashed in the bloody dust.

Then Ocnus of Falerii
    Rushed on the Roman Three;
And Lausulus of Urgo,
    The rover of the sea;
And Aruns of Volsinium,
    Who slew the great wild boar,
The great wild boar that had his den
Amidst the reeds of Cosa's fen,
And wasted fields, and slaughtered men,
    Along Albinia's shore.

Herminius smote down Aruns:
    Lartius laid Ocnus low:
Right to the heart of Lausulus
    Horatius sent a blow.
"Lie there," he cried, "fell pirate!
    No more, aghast and pale,
From Ostia's walls the crowd shall mark
The track of thy destroying bark.
No more Campania's hinds shall fly
To woods and caverns when they spy
    Thy thrice accursed sail."

But now no sound of laughter
　　Was heard among the foes.
A wild and wrathful clamor
　　From all the vanguard rose.
Six spears' lengths from the entrance
　　Halted that deep array,
And for a space no man came forth
　　To win the narrow way.

But hark! the cry is Astur:
　　And lo! the ranks divide;
And the great Lord of Luna
　　Comes with his stately stride.
Upon his ample shoulders
　　Clangs loud the four-fold shield,
And in his hand he shakes the brand
　　Which none but he can wield.

He smiled on those bold Romans
　　A smile serene and high;
He eyed the flinching Tuscans,
　　And scorn was in his eye.
Quoth he, "The she-wolf's litter
　　Stand savagely at bay:
But will ye dare to follow,
　　If Astur clears the way?"

Then, whirling up his broadsword
　　With both hands to the height,
He rushed against Horatius,
　　And smote with all his might.
With shield and blade Horatius
　　Right deftly turned the blow.
The blow, though turned, came yet too nigh;
It missed his helm, but gashed his thigh:
The Tuscans raised a joyful cry
　　To see the red blood flow.

He reeled, and on Herminius
　　He leaned one breathing-space;
Then, like a wild cat mad with wounds,
　　Sprang right at Astur's face.
Through teeth, and skull, and helmet,
　　So fierce a thrust he sped,
The good sword stood a hand-breadth out
　　Behind the Tuscan's head.

And the great Lord of Luna
　　Fell at that deadly stroke,
As falls on Mount Alvernus
　　A thunder-smitten oak.
Far o'er the crashing forest
　　The giant arms lie spread;
And the pale augurs, muttering low,
　　Gaze on the blasted head.

On Astur's throat Horatius
    Right firmly pressed his heels,
And thrice and four times tugged amain,
    Ere he wrenched out the steel.
"And see," he cried, "the welcome,
    Fair guests, that waits you here!
What noble Lucomo comes next,
    To taste our Roman cheer?"

But at this haughty challenge
    A sullen murmur ran,
Mingled of wrath, and shame, and dread,
    Along that glittering van.
There lacked not men of prowess,
    Nor men of lordly race;
For all Etruria's noblest
    Were round the fatal place.

Was none who would be foremost
    To lead such dire attack;
But those behind cried "Forward!"
    And those before cried "Back!"
And backward now and forward
    Wavers the deep array;
And on the tossing sea of steel,
To and fro the standards reel;
And the victorious trumpet-peal
    Dies fitfully away.

But meanwhile axe and lever
    Have manfully been plied,
And now the bridge hangs tottering
    Above the boiling tide.
"Come back, come back, Horatius!"
    Loud cried the Fathers all.
"Back, Lartius! back, Herminius!
    Back, ere the ruin fall!"

Back darted Spurius Lartius;
    Herminius darted back:
And, as they passed, beneath their feet
    They felt the timbers crack.
But when they turned their faces,
    And on the farther shore
Saw brave Horatius stand alone,
    They would have crossed once more.

Alone stood brave Horatius,
    But constant still in mind;
Thrice thirty thousand foes before,
    And the broad flood behind.
"Down with him!" cried false Sextus,
    With a smile on his pale face.
"Now yield thee," cried Lars Porsena,
    "Now yield thee to our grace."

Round turned he, as not deigning
    Those craven ranks to see;
Naught spake he to Lars Porsena,
    To Sextus naught spake he:
But he saw on Palatinus
    The white porch of his home;
And he spake to the noble river
    That rolls by the towers of Rome.

"Oh, Tiber! Father Tiber!
    To whom the Romans pray,
A Roman's life, a Roman's arms,
    Take thou in charge this day!"
So he spake, and speaking sheathed
    The good sword by his side,
And with his harness on his back,
    Plunged headlong in the tide.

No sound of joy or sorrow
    Was heard from either bank;
But friends and foes in dumb surprise,
With parted lips and straining eyes,
    Stood gazing where he sank;
And when above the surges
    They saw his crest appear,
All Rome sent forth a rapturous cry,
And even the ranks of Tuscany
    Could scarce forbear to cheer.

But fiercely ran the current,
  Swollen high by months of rain:
And fast his blood was flowing;
  And he was sore in pain,
And heavy with his armor,
  And spent with changing blows:
And oft they thought him sinking,
  But still again he rose.

Never, I ween, did swimmer,
  In such an evil case,
Struggle through such a raging flood
  Safe to the landing-place:
But his limbs were borne up bravely
  By the brave heart within,
And our good Father Tiber
  Bare bravely up his chin.

"Curse on him!" quoth false Sextus:
  "Will not the villain drown?
But for this stay, ere close of day
  We should have sacked the town!"
"Heaven help him!" quoth Lars Porsena,
  "And bring him safe to shore;
For such a gallant feat of arms
  Was never seen before."

And now he feels the bottom;
  Now on dry earth he stands;
Now round him throng the Fathers
  To press his gory hands;
And now, with shouts and clapping,
  And noise of weeping loud,
He enters through the River-gate,
  Borne by the joyous crowd.

They gave him of the corn-land
  That was of public right
As much as two strong oxen
  Could plough from morn till night;
And they made a molten image,
  And set it up on high,
And there it stands unto this day
  To witness if I lie.

It stands in the Comitium,
  Plain for all folk to see;
Horatius in his harness,
  Halting upon one knee:
And underneath is written,
  In letters all of gold,
How valiantly he kept the bridge
  In the brave days of old.

THOMAS BABINGTON MACAULAY

Remember

Remember me when I am gone away,
Gone far away into the silent land;
When you can no more hold me by the hand,
Nor I half turn to go, yet turning stay.
Remember me when no more, day by day,
You tell me of our future that you planned;
Only remember me; you understand
It will be late to counsel then or pray.

Yet if you should forget me for a while
And afterwards remember, do not grieve;
For if the darkness and corruption leave
A vestige of the thoughts that once I had,
Better by far you should forget and smile
Than that you should remember and be sad.

CHRISTINA ROSETTI

Death is a Door

Death is only an old door
Set in a garden wall;
On gentle hinges it gives, at dusk
When the thrushes call.

Along the lintel are green leaves,
Beyond the light lies still;
Very willing and weary feet
Go over that sill.

There is nothing to trouble any heart;
Nothing to hurt at all.
Death is only a quiet door
In an old wall.

NANCY BYRD TURNER

He Is Not Dead

I cannot say, and I will not say
That he is dead. He is just away.
With a cheery smile, and a wave of the hand,
He has wandered into an unknown land
And left us dreaming how very fair
It needs must be, since he lingers there.
And you—oh, you, who the wildest yearn
For an old-time step, and the glad return,
Think of him faring on, as dear
In the love of There as the love of Here.
Think of him still as the same. I say,
He is not dead—he is just away.

JAMES WHITCOMB RILEY

The Ballad of Reading Gaol

I never saw a man who looked
   With such a wistful eye
Upon that little tent of blue
   Which prisoners call the sky,
And at every drifting cloud that went
   With sails of silver by.

I walked, with other souls in pain,
   Within another ring,
And was wondering if the man had done
   A great or little thing,
When a voice behind me whispered low,
   "That fellow's got to swing."

Dear Christ! the very prison walls
   Suddenly seemed to reel,
And the sky above my head became
   Like a casque of scorching steel;
And, though I was a soul in pain,
   My pain I could not feel.

I only knew what hunted thought
    Quickened his step, and why
He looked upon the garish day
    With such a wistful eye;
The man had killed the thing he loved,
    And so he had to die.

Yet each man kills the thing he loves,
    By each let this be heard,
Some do it with a bitter look,
    Some with a flattering word,
The coward does it with a kiss,
    The brave man with a sword!

Some kill their love when they are young,
    And some when they are old;
Some strangle with the hands of Lust,
    Some with the hands of Gold:
The kindest use a knife, because
    The dead so soon grow cold.

Some love too little, some too long,
    Some sell, and others buy;
Some do the deed with many tears,
    And some without a sigh:
For each man kills the thing he loves,
    Yet each man does not die.

He does not die a death of shame
    On a day of dark disgrace,
Nor have a noose about his neck,
    Nor a cloth upon his face,
Nor drop feet foremost through the floor
    Into an empty space.

He does not sit with silent men
    Who watch him night and day;
Who watch him when he tries to weep,
    And when he tries to pray;
Who watch him lest himself should rob
    The prison of its prey.

He does not wake at dawn to see
    Dread figures throng his room,
The shivering Chaplain robed in white,
    The Sheriff stern with gloom,
And the Governor all in shiny black,
    With the yellow face of Doom.

He does not rise in piteous haste
    To put on convict-clothes,
While some coarse-mouthed Doctor gloats, and notes
    Each new and nerve-twitched pose,
Fingering a watch whose little ticks
    Are like horrible hammer-blows.

He does not know that sickening thirst
    That sands one's throat, before
The hangman with his gardener's gloves
    Slips through the padded door,
And binds one with three leathern thongs,
    That the throat may thirst no more.

He does not bend his head to hear
    The Burial Office read,
Nor, while the terror of his soul
    Tells him he is not dead,
Cross his own coffin, as he moves
    Into the hideous shed.

He does not stare upon the air
    Through a little roof of glass:
He does not pray with lips of clay
    For his agony to pass;
Nor feel upon his shuddering cheek
    That kiss of Caiaphas.

It is sweet to dance to violins
    When Love and Life are fair:
To dance to flutes, to dance to lutes
    Is delicate and rare:
But it is not sweet with nimble feet
    To dance upon the air!

OSCAR WILDE

In Memoriam

A late lark twitters from the quiet skies;
And from the west,
Where the sun, his day's work ended,
Lingers as in content,
There falls on the old, gray city
An influence luminous and serene,
A shining peace.

The smoke ascends
In a rosy-and-golden haze. The spires
Shine, and are changed. In the valley
Shadows rise. The lark sings on. The sun,
Closing his benediction,
Sinks, and the darkening air
Thrills with a sense of the triumphing night—
Night with her train of stars
And her great gift of sleep.

So be my passing!
My task accomplished and the long day done,
My wages taken, and in my heart
Some late lark singing,
Let me be gathered to the quiet west,
The sundown splendid and serene,
Death.

WILLIAM ERNEST HENLEY

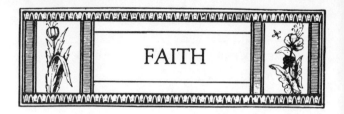

My Church

My church has but one temple,
    Wide as the world is wide,
Set with a million stars,
    Where a million hearts abide.

My church has no creed to bar
    A single brother man
But says, "Come thou and worship"
    To every one who can.

My church has no roof nor walls,
    Nor floors save the beautiful sod—
For fear, I would seem to limit
    The love of the illimitable God.

UNKNOWN. SIGNED E.O.G.

There Is No Unbelief

There is no unbelief;
Whoever plants a seed beneath the sod
And waits to see it push away the clod,
   He trusts in God.

There is no unbelief;
Whoever says, when clouds are in the sky,
"Be patient, heart; light breaketh by and by,"
   Trusts the Most High.

There is no unbelief;
Whoever sees, 'neath winter's field of snow,
The silent harvest of the future grow—
   God's power must know.

There is no unbelief;
Whoever lies down on his couch to sleep,
Content to lock each sense in slumber deep,
   Knows God will keep.

There is no unbelief;
The heart that looks on when dear eyelids close,
And dares to live when life has only woes,
   God's comfort knows.

LIZZIE YORK CASE

A Poison Tree

I was angry with my friend:
I told my wrath, my wrath did end.
I was angry with my foe:
I told it not, my wrath did grow.

And I watered it in fears
Night and morning with my tears,
And I sunned it with smiles
And with soft deceitful wiles.

And it grew both day and night,
Till it bore an apple bright,
And my foe beheld it shine,
And he knew that it was mine—

And into my garden stole
When the night had veiled the pole;
In the morning, glad, I see
My foe outstretched beneath the tree.

WILLIAM BLAKE

Around the Corner

Around the corner I have a friend,
In this great city that has no end;
Yet days go by, and weeks rush on,
And before I know it a year is gone,
And I never see my old friend's face,
For Life is a swift and terrible race.
He knows I like him just as well
As in the days when I rang his bell
And he rang mine. We were younger then,
And now we are busy, tired men:
Tired with trying to make a name.
"Tomorrow," I say, "I will call on Jim,
Just to show that I'm thinking of him."
But tomorrow comes—and tomorrow goes,
And the distance between us grows and grows
Around the corner!—yet miles away. . . .
"Here's a telegram, sir. . . ."

"Jim died today."

And that's what we get, and deserve in the end:
Around the corner, a vanished friend.

CHARLES HANSON TOWNE

Friendship

Friendship needs no studied phrases,
    Polished face, or winning wiles;
Friendship deals no lavish praises,
    Friendship dons no surface smiles.

Friendship follows Nature's diction,
    Shuns the blandishments of Art,
Boldly severs truth from fiction,
    Speaks the language of the heart.

Friendship favors no condition,
    Scorns a narrow-minded creed,
Lovingly fulfills its mission,
    Be it word or be it deed.

Friendship cheers the faint and weary,
    Makes the timid spirit brave,
Warns the erring, lights the dreary,
    Smooths the passage to the grave.

Friendship—pure, unselfish friendship,
    All through life's allotted span,
Nurtures, strengthens, widens, lengthens,
    Man's relationship with man.

AUTHOR UNKNOWN

Fellowship

When a feller hasn't got a cent
And is feelin' kind of blue,
And the clouds hang thick and dark
And won't let the sunshine thro'
It's a great thing, oh my brethren,
For a feller just to lay
His hand upon your shoulder
   in a friendly sort o' way.

It make a man feel queerish,
It makes the tear-drops start.
And you kind o' feel a flutter
In the region of your heart.
You can't look up and meet his eye,
You don't know what to say
When a hand is on your shoulder
   in a friendly sort o' way.

Oh this world's a curious compound
With its honey and its gall;
Its cares and bitter crosses,
But a good world after all.
And a good God must have made it,
Leastwise that is what I say,
When a hand is on your shoulder
   in a friendly sort o' way.

AUTHOR UNKNOWN

To Know All Is
To Forgive All

If I knew you and you knew me—
If both of us could clearly see,
And with an inner sight divine
The meaning of your heart and mine—
I'm sure that we would differ less
And clasp our hands in friendliness;
Our thoughts would pleasantly agree
If I knew you, and you knew me.

If I knew you and you knew me,
As each one knows his own self, we
Could look each other in the face
And see therein a truer grace.

Life has so many hidden woes,
So many thorns for every rose;
The "why" of things our hearts would see,
If I knew you and you knew me.

NIXON WATERMAN

GRIEF

Anthem for Doomed Youth

What passing-bells for these who die as cattle?
Only the monstrous anger of the guns.
Only the stuttering rifles' rapid rattle
Can patter out their hasty orisons.
No mockeries for them; no prayers nor bells,
Nor any voice of mourning save the choirs,—
The shrill, demented choirs of wailing shells;
And bugles calling for them from sad shires.

What candles may be held to speed them all?
Not in the hands of boys, but in their eyes
Shall shine the holy glimmers of good-bys.
The pallor of girls' brows shall be their pall;
Their flowers the tenderness of patient minds,
And each slow dusk a drawing-down of blinds.

WILFRED OWEN

Annabel Lee

It was many and many a year ago,
  In a kingdom by the sea,
That a maiden there lived whom you may know
  By the name of Annabel Lee;—
And this maiden she lived with no other thought
  Than to love and be loved by me.

She was a child and I was a child,
  In this kingdom by the sea,
But we loved with a love that was more than love—
  I and my Annabel Lee—
With a love that the winged seraphs of Heaven
  Coveted her and me.

And this was the reason that, long ago,
  In this kingdom by the sea,
A wind blew out of a cloud, by night
  Chilling my Annabel Lee;
So that her highborn kinsmen came
  And bore her away from me,
To shut her up in a sepulchre
  In this kingdom by the sea.

The angels, not half so happy in Heaven,
    Went envying her and me:
Yes! that was the reason (as all men know,
    In this kingdom by the sea)
That the wind came out of the cloud, chilling
    And killing my Annabel Lee.

But our love it was stronger by far than the love
    Of those who were older than we—
    Of many far wiser than we—
And neither the angels in Heaven above
    Nor the demons down under the sea,
Can ever dissever my soul from the soul
    Of the beautiful Annabel Lee:—

For the moon never beams without bringing me
        dreams
    Of the beautiful Annabel Lee;
And the stars never rise but I see the bright eyes
    Of the beautiful Annabel Lee;
And so, all the night-tide, I lie down by the side
Of my darling, my darling, my life and my bridge,
    In her sepulchre there by the sea—
    In her tomb by the sounding sea.

EDGAR ALLAN POE

Joseph Rodman Drame

Green be the turf above thee,
    Friend of my better days!
None knew thee but to love thee,
    Nor named thee but to praise.

Tears fell, when thou wert dying,
    From eyes unused to weep,
And long, where thou art lying,
    Will tears the cold turf steep.

When hearts, whose truth was proven,
    Like thine, are laid in earth,
There should a wreath be woven
    To tell the world their worth;

And I, who woke each morrow
    To clasp thy hand in mine,
Who shared thy joy and sorrow,
    Whose weal and woe were thine,

It should be mine to braid it
    Around thy faded brow,
But I've in vain essayed it,
    And feel I cannot now.

While memory bids me weep thee,
    Nor thoughts nor words are free,
The grief is fixed too deeply
    That mourns a man like thee.

FITZ-GREENE HALLECK

Of De Witt Williams on His Way to Lincoln Cemetery

He was born in Alabama.
He was bred in Illinois.
He was nothing but a
Plain black boy.

Swing low swing low sweet sweet chariot.
Nothing but a plain black boy.

Drive him past the Pool Hall.
Drive him past the Show.
Blind within his casket,
But maybe he will know.

Down through Forty-seventh Street:
Underneath the L,
And Northwest Corner, Prairie,
That he loved so well.

Don't forget the Dance Halls—
Warwick and Savoy,
Where he picked his women, where
He drank his liquid joy.

Born in Alabama.
Bred in Illinois.
He was nothing but a
Plain black boy.

Swing low swing low sweet sweet chariot.
Nothing but a plain black boy.

GWENDOLYN BROOKS

Home They Brought Her Warrior Dead

Home they brought her warrior dead:
    She nor swooned, nor uttered cry:
All her maidens, watching, said,
    "She must weep or she will die."

Then they praised him, soft and low,
    Called him worthy to be loved,
Truest friend and noblest foe;
    Yet she neither spoke nor moved.

Stole a maiden from her place,
    Lightly to the warrior stept,
Took the face-cloth from the face;
    Yet she neither moved nor wept.

Rose a nurse of ninety years,
    Set his child upon her knee—
Like summer tempest came her tears—
    "Sweet my child, I live for thee."

ALFRED, LORD TENNYSON

Patterns

I walk down the garden-paths,
And all the daffodils
Are blowing, and the bright blue squills.
I walk down the patterned garden-paths
In my stiff, brocaded gown.
With my powdered hair and jeweled fan,
I too am a rare
Pattern. As I wander down
The garden-paths.

My dress is richly figured,
And the train
Makes a pink and silver strain
On the gravel, and the thrift
Of the borders.
Just a plate of current fashion,
Tripping by in high-heeled, ribboned shoes.
Not a softness anywhere about me,
Only whalebone and brocade.
And I sink on a seat in the shade
Of a lime-tree. For my passion
Wars against the stiff brocade.
The daffodils and squills
Flutter in the breeze
As they please.

And I weep;
For the lime-tree is in blossom
And one small flower has dropped upon my bosom.

And the plashing of waterdrops
In the marble fountain
Comes down the garden-paths.
The dripping never stops.
Underneath my stiffened gown
Is the softness of a woman bathing in a marble basin,
A basin in the midst of hedges grown
So thick, she cannot see her lover hiding,
But she guesses he is near,
And the sliding of the water
Seems the stroking of a dear
Hand upon her.
What is Summer in a fine brocaded gown!
I should like to see it lying in a heap upon the
          ground.
All the pink and silver crumpled up on the ground.

I would be the pink and silver as I ran along the
          paths,
And he would stumble after,
Bewildered by my laughter.
I should see the sun flashing from his sword-hilt and
          the buckles on his shoes.
I would choose

To lead him in a maze along the patterned paths,
A bright and laughing maze for my heavy-booted lover.
Till he caught me in the shade,
And the buttons of his waistcoat bruised my body as
      he clasped me,
Aching, melting, unafraid.
With the shadows of the leaves and the sundrops,
And the plopping of the waterdrops,
All about us in the open afternoon—
I am very like to swoon
With the weight of this brocade,
For the sun sifts through the shade.

Underneath the fallen blossom
In my bosom
Is a letter I had hid.
It was brought to me this morning by a rider from the
      Duke.
"Madam, we regret to inform you that Lord Hartwell
Died in action Thursday sen'night."
As I read it in the white, morning sunlight,
The letters squirmed like snakes.
"Any answer, Madam?" said my footman.
"No," I told him.
"See that the messenger takes some refreshment.
No, no answer."
And I walked into the garden,
Up and down the patterned paths,

In my stiff, correct brocade.
The blue and yellow flowers stood up proudly
       in the sun,
Each one.
I stood upright too,
Held rigid to the pattern
By the stiffness of my grown;
Up and down I walked,
Up and down.

In a month he would have been my husband.
In a month, here, underneath this lime,
We would have broke the pattern;
He for me, and I for him,
He as Colonel, I as Lady,
On this shady seat.
He had a whim
That sunlight carried blessing.
And I answered, "It shall be as you have said."
Now he is dead.

In Summer and in Winter I shall walk
Up and down
The patterned garden-paths
In my stiff, brocaded gown.
The squills and daffodils
Will give place to pillared roses, and to asters,
       and to snow.

I shall go
Up and down
In my gown.
Gorgeously arrayed,
Boned and stayed.
And the softness of my body will be guarded
        from embrace
By each button, hook, and lace.
For the man who should loose me is dead,
Fighting with the Duke in Flanders,
In a pattern called a war.
Christ! What are patterns for?

AMY LOWELL

HOME

Home, Sweet Home

'Mid pleasures and palaces though we may roam,
Be it ever so humble, there's no place like home;
A charm from the sky seems to hallow us there,
Which, seek through the world, is ne'er met with
elsewhere.
Home, home, sweet, sweet home!
There's no place like home, oh, there's no place like
home!

An exile from home, splendor dazzles in vain;
Oh, give me my lowly thatched cottage again!
The birds singing gayly, that came at my call—
Give me them—and the peace of mind, dearer than
all!
Home, home, sweet, sweet home!
There's no place like home, oh, there's no place like
home!

I gaze on the moon as I tread the drear wild,
And feel that my mother now thinks of her child,
As she looks on that moon from our own cottage
door
Thro' the woodbine, whose fragrance shall cheer me
no more.
Home, home, sweet, sweet home!
There's no place like home, oh, there's no place like
home!

How sweet 'tis to sit 'neath a fond father's smile,
And the caress of a mother to soothe and beguile!
Let others delight 'mid new pleasure to roam,
But give me, oh, give me, the pleasures of home,
Home, home, sweet, sweet home!
There's no place like home, oh, there's no place like
home!

To thee I'll return, overburdened with care;
The heart's dearest solace will smile on me there;
No more from that cottage again will I roam;
Be it ever so humble, there's no place like home.
Home, home, sweet, sweet home!
There's no place like home, oh, there's no place like
home!

JOHN HOWARD PAYNE

A Prayer For A Little Home

God send us a little home,
To come back to, when we roam.

Low walls and fluted tiles,
Wide windows, a view for miles.

Red firelight and deep chairs,
Small white beds upstairs—

Great talk in little nooks,
Dim colors, rows of books.

One picture on each wall,
Not many things at all.

God send us a little ground,
Tall trees stand round.

Homely flowers in brown sod,
Overhead, thy stars, O God.

God bless thee, when winds blow,
Our home, and all we know.

FLORENCE BONE

Home Is Where There Is One To Love Us

Home's not merely four square walls,
Though with pictures hung and gilded;
Home is where Affection calls—
Filled with shrines the Hearth had builded!
Home! Go watch the faithful dove,
Sailing 'neath the heaven above us.
Home is where there's one to love!
Home is where there's one to love us.

Home's not merely roof and room,
It needs something to endear it;
Home is where the heart can bloom,
Where there's some kind lip to cheer it!
What is home with none to meet,
None to welcome, none to greet us?
Home is sweet, and only sweet,
Where there's one we love to meet us!

CHARLES SWAIN

INSPIRATION

Battle-Hymn of the Republic

Mine eyes have seen the glory of the coming of the
     Lord:
He is trampling out the vintage where the grapes of
     wrath are stored;
He hath loosed the fateful lightning of his terrible
     swift sword:
  His truth is marching on.

I have seen him in the watch-fires of a hundred
     circling camps;
They have builded him an altar in the evening dews
     and damps;
I can read his righteous sentence by the dim and
     flaring lamps:
  His day is marching on.

. as fiery gospel, writ in burnished rows of
el:
eal with my contemners, so with you my
ace shall deal;
lero, born of woman, crush the serpent with
s heel,
  Since God is marching on."

He has sounded forth the trumpet that shall never call
      retreat;
He is sifting out the hearts of men before his
      judgment-seat:
O, be swift, my soul, to answer him! be jubilant, my
      feet!
  Our God is marching on.

In the beauty of the lilies Christ was born across the
      sea,
With a glory in his bosom that transfigures you and
      me;
As he died to make men holy, let us die to make men
      free,
  While God is marching on.

JULIA WARD HOWE

It Couldn't Be Done

Somebody said that it couldn't be done,
    But he with a chuckle replied
That "maybe it couldn't," but he would be one
    Who wouldn't say so till he'd tried.
So he buckled right in with the trace of a grin
    On his face. If he worried he hid it.
He started to sing as he tackled the thing
    That couldn't be done, and he did it.

Somebody scoffed: "Oh, you'll never do that;
    At least no one ever has done it";
But he took off his coat and he took off his hat,
    And the first thing we knew he'd begun it.
With a lift of his chin and a bit of a grin,
    Without any doubting or quiddit,
He started to sing as he tackled the thing
    That couldn't be done, and he did it.

There are thousands to tell you it cannot be done,
    There are thousands to prophesy failure;
There are thousands to point out to you, one by one,
    The dangers that wait to assail you.
But just buckle in with a bit of a grin,
    Just take off your coat and go to it;
Just start to sing as you tackle the thing
    That "cannot be done," and you'll do it.

EDGAR A. GUEST

Carry On!

It's easy to fight when everything's right,
And you're mad with the thrill and the glory;
It's easy to cheer when victory's near,
And wallow in fields that are gory.
It's a different song when everything's wrong,
When you're feeling infernally mortal;
When it's ten against one, and hope there is none,
Buck up, little soldier, and chortle:

Carry on! Carry on!
There isn't much punch in your blow.
You're glaring and staring and hitting out blind;
You're muddy and bloody, but never you mind.
Carry on! Carry on!
You haven't the ghost of a show.
It's looking like death, but while you've a breath,
Carry on, my son! Carry on!

And so in the strife of the battle of life
It's easy to fight when you're winning;
It's easy to slave, and starve and be brave,
When the dawn of success is beginning.
But the man who can meet despair and defeat
With a cheer, there's the man of God's choosing;
The man who can fight to Heaven's own height
Is the man who can fight when he's losing.

Carry on! Carry on!
Things never were looming so black.
But show that you haven't a cowardly streak,
And though you're unlucky you never are weak.
Carry on! Carry on!
Brace up for another attack.
It's looking like hell, but—you never can tell:
Carry on, old man! Carry on!

There are some who drift out in the deserts of doubt,
And some who in brutishness wallow;
There are others, I know, who in piety go
Because of a Heaven to follow.
But to labour with zest, and to give of your best,
For the sweetness and joy of the giving;
To help folks along with a hand and a song;
Why, there's the real sunshine of living.

Carry on! Carry on!
Fight the good fight and true;
Believe in your mission, greet life with a cheer;
There's big work to do, and that's why you are here.
Carry on! Carry on!
Let the world be the better for you;
And at last when you die, let this be your cry:
Carry on, my soul! Carry on!

ROBERT SERVICE

Say Not the Struggle Naught Availeth

Say not the struggle naught availeth,
   The labor and the wounds are vain,
The enemy faints not, nor faileth,
   And as things have been they remain.

If hopes were dupes, fears may be liars;
   It may be, in yon smoke conceal'd,
Your comrades chase e'en now the fliers,
   And, but for you, possess the field.

For while the tired waves, vainly breaking,
   Seem here no painful inch to gain,
Far back, through creeks and inlets making,
   Comes silent, flooding in, the main.

And not by eastern windows only,
   When daylight comes, comes in the light;
In front the sun climbs slow, how slowly.
   But westward, look, the land is bright

ARTHUR CLOUGH

Hold Fast Your Dreams

Hold fast your dreams!
Within your heart
Keep one still, secret spot
Where dreams may go,
And, sheltered so,
May thrive and grow
Where doubt and fear are not.
O keep a place apart,
Within your heart,
For little dreams to go!

Think still of lovely things that are not true.
Let wish and magic work at will in you.
Be sometimes blind to sorrow. Make believe!
Forget the calm that lies
In disillusioned eyes.
Though we all know that we must die,
Yet you and I
May walk like gods and be
Even now at home in immortality.

We see so many ugly things—
Deceits and wrongs and quarrelings;
We know, alas! we know
How quickly fade
The color in the west,
The bloom upon the breast
And youth's blind hour.
Yet keep within your heart
A place apart
Where little dreams may go,
May thrive and grow.
Hold fast—hold fast your dreams!

LOUISE DRISCOLL

LOVE

The Night Has a Thousand Eyes

The night has a thousand eyes,
    And the day but one;
Yet the light of the bright world dies
    With the dying sun.

The mind has a thousand eyes,
    And the heart but one;
Yet the light of a whole life dies
    When love is done.

FRANCIS WILLIAM BOURDILLON

If Love Be Love

In Love, if Love be Love, if Love be ours,
Faith and unfaith can ne'er be equal powers:
Unfaith in aught is want of faith in all.

It is the little rift within the lute,
That by and by will make the music mute,
And ever widening slowly silence all.

The little rift within the lover's lute
Or little pitted speck in garnered fruit,
That rotting inward slowly moulders all.

It is not worth the keeping: let it go:
But shall it? answer, darling, answer, no.
And trust me not at all or all in all.

ALFRED, LORD TENNYSON

Midsummer

You loved me for a little,
　　Who could not love me long;
You gave me wings of gladness
　　And lent my spirit song.

You loved me for an hour
　　But only with your eyes;
Your lips I could not capture
　　By storm or by surprise.

Your mouth that I remember
　　With rush of sudden pain
As one remembers starlight
　　Or roses after rain . . .

Out of a world of laughter
　　Suddenly I am sad. . . .
Day and night it haunts me,
　　The kiss I never had.

SYDNEY KING RUSSELL

Need of Loving

Folk need a lot of loving in the morning;
 The day is all before, with cares beset—
The cares we know, and they that give no warning;
 Fr love is God's own antidote for fret.

Folk need a heap of loving at the noontime—
 In the battle lull, the moment snatch from
 strife—
Halfway between the waking and the croon time,
 While bickering and worriment are rife.

Folk hunger so for loving at the nighttime,
 When wearily they take them home to rest—
At slumber song and turning-out-the-light time—
 Of all the times for lovinmg, that's the best.

Folk want a lot of loving every minute—
 The sympathy of others and their smile!
Till life's end, from the moment they begin it,
 Folks need a lot of loving all the while.

STRICKLAND GILLILAN

The Power of the Dog

There is sorrow enough in the natural way
From men and women to fill our day;
And when we are certain of sorrow in store,
Why do we always arrange for more?
Brothers and Sisters, I bid you beware
Of giving your heart to a dog to tear.

Buy a pup and your money will buy
Love unflinching that cannot lie—
Perfect passion and worship fed
By a kick in the ribs or a pat on the head.
Nevertheless it is hardly fair
To risk your heart for a dog to tear.

When the fourteen years which Nature permits
Are closing in asthma, or tumour, or fits,
And the vet's unspoken prescription runs
To lethal chambers or loaded guns,
Then you will find—it's your own affair—
But . . . you've given your heart to a dog to tear.

When the body that lived at your single will,
With its whimper of welcome, is stilled (how still!);
When the spirit that answered your every mood
Is gone—wherever it goes—for good,
You will discover how much you care,
And will give your heart to a dog to tear.

We've sorrow enough in the natural way,
When it comes to burying Christian clay.
Our loves are not given, but only lent,
At compound interest of cent per cent.
Though it is not always the case, I believe,
That the longer we've kept 'em, the more do we
        grieve:
For, when debts are payable, right or wrong,
A short-time loan is as bad as a long—
So why in—Heaven (before we are there)
Should we give our hearts to a dog to tear?

RUDYARD KIPLING

103

MORTALITY

The House on the Hill

They are all gone away,
    The House is shut and still,
There is nothing more to say.

Through broken walls and gray
    The winds blow bleak and shrill;
They are all gone away.

Nor is there one today
    To speak them good or ill:
There is nothing more to say.

Why is it then we stray
    Around that sunken sill?
They are all gone away,

And our poor fancy-play
    For them is wasted skill:
There is nothing more to say.

There is ruin and decay
    In the House on the Hill:
They are all gone away,
There is nothing more to say.

EDWIN ARLINGTON ROBINSON

When the Lamp Is Shattered

When the lamp is shattered,
The light in the dust lies dead;
When the cloud is scattered,
The rainbow's glory is shed;
When the lute is broken,
Sweet tones are remembered not;
When the lips have spoken,
Loved accents are soon forgot.

As music and splendor
Survive not the lamp and the lute,
The heart's echoes render
No song when the spirit is mute:—
No song but sad dirges,
Like the wind through a ruined cell,
Or the mournful surges
That ring the dead seaman's knell.

When hearts have once mingled,
Love first leaves the well-built nest;
The weak one is singled
To endure what it once possessed.
O Love! who bewailest
The frailty of all things here,
Why choose you the frailest
For your cradle, your home, and your bier?

Its passions will rock thee,
As the storms rock the ravens on high;
Bright reason will mock thee,
Like the sun from a wintry sky.
From thy nest every rafter
Will rot, and thine eagle home
Leave the naked to laughter,
When leaves fall and cold winds come.

PERCY BYSSHE SHELLEY

To the Virgins to Make Much of Time

Gather ye rose-buds while ye may,
  Old Time is still a-flying:
And this same flower that smiles today,
  Tomorrow will be dying.

The glorious lamp of heaven, the Sun,
  The higher he's a-getting
The sooner will his race be run,
  And nearer he's to setting.

That age is best which is the first,
  When youth and blood are warmer;
But being spent, the worse, and worst
  Times, still succeed the former.

Then be not coy, but use your time;
  And while ye may, go marry:
For having lost but once your prime,
  You may for ever tarry.

ROBERT HERRICK

MOTHER

A Wonderful Mother

God made a wonderful mother,
A mother who never grows old;
He made her smile of the sunshine,
And He molded her heart of pure gold;
In her eyes He placed bright shining stars,
In her cheeks, fair roses you see;
God made a wonderful mother,
And He gave that dear mother to me.

PAT O'REILLY

Rock Me to Sleep

Backward, turn backward, O Time, in your flight,
Make me a child again just for to-night!
Mother, come back from the echoless shore,
Take me again to your heart as of yore;
Kiss from my forehead the furrows of care,
Smooth the few silver threads out of my hair;
Over my slumbers your loving watch keep—
Rock me to sleep, mother—rock me to sleep!

Backward, flow backward, O tide of the years!
I am so weary of toil and of tears—
Toil without recompense, tears all in vain—
Take them and give me my childhood again!
I have grown weary of dust and decay,
Weary of flinging my soul-wealth away,
Weary of sowing for others to reap—
Rock me to sleep, mother—rock me to sleep!

Tired of the hollow, the base, the untrue,
Mother, O mother, my heart calls for you!
Many a summer the grass has grown green,
Blossomed and faded, our faces between;
Yet, with strong yearning and passionate pain,
Long I to-night for your presence again;
Come from the silence so long and so deep—
Rock me to sleep, mother—rock me to sleep!

Over my heart in the days that are flown,
No love like mother-love ever has shone;
No other worship abides and endures,
Faithful, unselfish, and patient, like yours;
None like a mother can charm away pain
From the sick soul and the world-weary brain;
Slumber's soft calms o'er my heavy lids creep—
Rock me to sleep, mother—rock me to sleep!

Come, let your brown hair, just lighted with gold,
Fall on your shoulders again as of old;
Let it drop over my forehead to-night,
Shading my faint eyes away from the light;
For with its sunny-edge shadows once more,
Haply will throng the sweet visions of yore;
Lovingly, softly, its bright billows sweep—
Rock me to sleep, mother—rock me to sleep!

Mother, dear mother, the years have been long
Since I last listened your lullaby song;
Sing, then, and unto my soul it shall seem
Womanhood's years have been only a dream.
Clasped to your heart in a loving embrace,
With your light lashes just sweeping my face,
Never hereafter to wake or to weep—
Rock me to sleep, mother—rock me to sleep!

ELIZABETH AKERS

The Isles of Greece

The isles of Greece! the isles of Greece
　　Where burning Sappho loved and sung,
Where grew the arts of war and peace,
　　Where Delos rose, and Phoebus sprung!
Eternal summer gilds them yet,
But all, except their sun, is set.

The mountains look on Marathon—
　　And Marathon looks on the sea;
And musing there an hour alone,
　　I dream'd that Greece might still be free;
For standing on the Persians' grave,
I could not deem myself a slave.

GEORGE GORDON, LORD BYRON

America the Beautiful

O beautiful for spacious skies,
 For amber waves of grain,
For purple mountain majesties
 Above the fruited plain!
America! America!
 God shed His grace on thee
And crown thy good with brotherhood
 From sea to shining sea!

O beautiful for pilgrim feet,
 Whose stern, impassioned stress
A thoroughfare for freedom beat
 Across the wilderness!
America! America!
 God mend thine every flaw,
Confirm thy soul in self-control,
 Thy liberty in law!

O beautiful for heroes proved
    In liberating strife,
Who more than self their country loved,
    And mercy more than life!
America! America!
    May God thy gold refine,
Till all success be nobleness
    And every gain divine!

O beautiful for patriot dream
    That sees beyond the years
Thine alabaster cities gleam
    Undimmed by human tears!
America! America!
    God shed His grace on thee,
And crown thy good with brotherhood
    From sea to shining sea!

KATHARINE LEE BATES

The Charge of the Light Brigade

Half a league, half a league,
  Half a league onward,
All in the valley of Death
Rode the six hundred.
"Forward, the Light Brigade!
Charge for the guns," he said:
Into the valley of Death
  Rode the six hundred.

"Forward, the Light Brigade!"
Was there a man dismay'd?
Not tho' the soldier knew
  Someone had blunder'd:
Theirs not to make reply,
Theirs not to reason why,
Theirs but to do and die:
Into the valley of Death
  Rode the six hundred.

Cannon to right of them,
cannon to left of them,
Cannon in front of them
  Volley'd and thunder'd;
Storm'd at with shot and shell,
Boldly they rode and well,

Into the jaws of Death,
Into the mouth of Hell
  Rode the six hundred.

Flash'd all their sabers bare,
Flash'd as they turn'd in air
Sabring the gunners there,
Charging an army, while
  All the world wonder'd:
Plung'd in the battery-smoke
Right thro' the line they broke;
Cossack and Russian
Reel'd from the saber-stroke
  Shatter'd and sunder'd.
Then they rode back, but not,
  Not the six hundred.

When can their glory fade?
O the wild charge they made!
  All the world wonder'd.
Honor the charge they made!
Honor the Light Brigade,
  Noble six hundred!

ALFRED, LORD TENNYSON

PHILOSOPHY

From Evangeline

Talk not of wasted affection! affection never was
      wasted;
If it enrich not the heart of another, its waters,
      returning
Back to their springs, like the rain, shall fill them full
      of refreshment:
That which the fountain sends forth returns again to
      the fountain.

FROM "EVANGELINE" BY HENRY WADSWORTH LONGFELLOW

Happiness

Happiness is like a crystal,
Fair and exquisite and clear,
Broken in a million pieces,
Shattered, scattered far and near.
Now and then along life's pathway,
Lo! some shining fragments fall;
But there are so many pieces
No one ever finds them all.

You may find a bit of beauty,
Or an honest share of wealth,
While another just beside you
Fathers honor, love or health.
Vain to choose or grasp unduly,
Broken is the perfect ball;
And there are so many pieces
No one ever finds them all.

Yet the wise as on they journey
Treasure every fragment clear,
Fit them as they may together,
Imaging the shattered sphere,
Learning ever to be thankful,
Though their share of it is small;
For it has so many pieces
No one ever finds them all.

PRISCILLA LEONARD

Brahma

If the red slayer think he slays,
　Or if the slain think he is slain,
They know not well the subtle ways
　I keep, and pass, and turn again.

Far or forgot to me is near;
　Shadow and sunlight are the same;
The vanished gods to me appear;
　And one to me are shame and fame.

They reckon ill who leave me out;
　When me they fly, I am the wings;
I am the doubter and the doubt,
　And I the hymn the Brahmin sings.

The strong gods pine for my abode,
　And pine in vain the sacred Seven;
But thou, meek lover of the good!
　Find me, and turn thy back on heaven.

RALPH WALDO EMERSON

Cool Tombs

When Abraham Lincoln was shoveled into the tombs,
    he forgot the copperheads and the assassin . . .
    in the dust, in the cool tombs.

And Ulysses Grant lost all thought of con men and
    Wall Street, cash and collateral turned ashes
    . . . in the dust, in the cool tombs.

Pocahontas' body, lovely as a poplar, sweet as a red
    haw in November or a pawpaw in May, did
    she wonder? does she remember? . . . in the
    dust, in the cool tombs?

Take any streetful of people buying clothes and
    groceries, cheering a hero or throwing confetti
    and blowing tin horns . . . tell me if the lovers
    are losers . . . tell me if any get more than the
    lovers . . . in the dust . . . in the cool tombs.

CARL SANDBURG

Don't Give Up

'Twixt failure and success the point's so fine
Men sometimes know not when they touch the line,
Just when the pearl was waiting one more plunge,
How many a struggler has thrown up the sponge!
Then take this honey from the bitterest cup:
"There is no failure save in giving up!"

AUTHOR UNKNOWN

Stanzas from the Kasidah

Friends of my youth, a last adieu!
   Haply some day we meet again;
Yet ne'er the self-same men shall meet;
   The years shall make us other men:

Fie, fie! you visionary things,
   Ye motes that dance in sunny glow,
Who base and build Eternities
   On briefest moment here below;

Who pass through Life like caged birds,
   The captives of a despot will;
Still wond'ring How and When and Why,
   And Whence and Whither, wond'ring still;

Who knows not Whence he came nor Why,
   Who kens not Whither bound and When,
Yet such is Allah's choicest gift,
   The blessing dreamt by foolish men;

Hardly we learn to wield the blade
    Before the wrist grows stiff and old;
Hardly we learn to ply the pen
    Ere Thought and Fancy faint with cold.

When swift the Camel-rider spans
    The howling waste, by Kismet sped,
And of his Magic Wand a wave
    Hurries the quick to join the dead.

How Thought is impotent to divine
    The secret which the gods defend,
The Why of birth and life and death,
    That Isis-veil no hand may rend.

O the dread pathos of our lives!
    How durst thou, Allah, thus to play
With Love, Affection, Friendship,
    All that shows the god in mortal clay.

Cease, Man, to mourn, to weep, to wail;
    Enjoy thy shining hour of sun;
We dance along Death's icy brink,
    But is the dance less full of fun?

How shall the Shown pretend to ken
    Aught of the Showman or the Show?
Why meanly bargain to believe,
    Which only means thou ne'er canst know?

There is no Good, there is no Bad;
    These be the whims of mortal will:
What works me weal that call I "good,"
    What harms and hurts I hold as "ill:"

They change with place, they shift with race;
    And, in the veriest span of Time,
Each Vice has won a Virtue's crown;
    All good was banned as Sin or Crime:

All Faith is false, all Faith is true:
    Truth is the shattered mirror strown
In myriad bits; while each believes
    His little bit the whole to own.

What is the Truth? was askt of yore.
    Reply all object Truth is one
As twain of halves aye makes as whole;
    The moral Truth for all is none.

With God's foreknowledge man's free will!
    What monster-growth of human brain,
What powers of light shall ever pierce
    This puzzle dense with words inane?

There is no Heaven, there is no Hell;
    These be the dreams of baby minds;
Tools of the wily Fetisheer,
    To 'fright the fools his cunning blinds.

Who drinks one bowl hath scant delight;
　　To poorest passion he was born;
Who drains the score must e'er expect
　　To rue the headache of the morn.

From self-approval seek applause:
　　What ken not men thou kennest, thou!
Spurn ev'ry idol others raise:
　　Before thine own Ideal bow:

Be thine own Deus: Make self free,
　　Liberal as the circling air:
Thy Thought to thee an Empire be;
　　Break every prisoning lock and bar:

OF SIR RICHARD F. BURTON

Ozymandias

I met a traveler from an antique land,
Who said: Two vast and trunkless legs of stone
Stand in the desert. Near them, on the sand,
Half sunk, a shattered visage lies, whose frown,
And wrinkled lip, and sneer of cold command,
Tell that its sculptor well those passions read,
Which yet survive, stamped on these lifeless things,
The hand that mocked them, and the heart that fed:
And on the pedestal these words appear:
"My name is Ozymandias, King of Kings:
Look on my works, ye Mighty, and despair!"
Nothing beside remains. Round the decay
Of that colossal wreck, boundless and bare
The lone and level sands stretch far away.

PERCY BYSSHE SHELLEY

The World Is Too Much With Us

The world is too much with us; late and soon,
Getting and spending, we lay waste our powers:
Little we see in Nature that is ours;
We have given our hearts away, a sordid boon!
The sea that bares her bosom to the moon;
The winds that will be howling at all hours,
And are up-gathered now like sleeping flowers;
For this, for everything, we are out of tune;
It moves us not.—Great God! I'd rather be
A pagan suckled in a creed outworn.
So might I, standing on this pleasant lea,
Have glimpses that would make me less forlorn;
Have sight of Proteus rising from the sea;
Or hear old Triton blow his wreathed horn.

WILLIAM WORDSWORTH

Vitae Summa Brevis

They are not long, the weeping and the laughter,
    Love and desire and hate;
I think they have no portion in us after
      We pass the gate.

They are not long, the days of wine and roses:
    Out of a misty dream
Our path emerges for a while, then closes
      Within a dream.

ERNEST DOWSON

Money

When I had money, money, O!
    I knew no joy till I went poor;
For many a false man as a friend
    Came knocking all day at my door.

Then felt I like a child that holds
    A trumpet that he must not blow
Because a man is dead; I dared
    Not speak to let this false world know.

Much have I thought of life, and seen
    How poor men's hearts are ever light;
And how their wives do hum like bees
    About their work from morn till night.

So, when I hear these poor ones laugh,
    And see the rich ones coldly frown—
Poor men, think I, need not go up
    So much as rich men should come down.

When I had money, money, O!
    My many friends proved all untrue;
But now I have no money, O!
    My friends are real, though very few.

WILLIAM HENRY DAVIES

Ulysses

It little profits that an idle king,
By this still hearth, among these barren crags,
Matched with an aged wife, I mete and dole
Unequal laws unto a savage race,
That hoard, and sleep, and feed, and know not me.
I cannot rest from travel: I will drink
Life to the lees: all times I have enjoyed
Greatly, have suffered greatly, both with those
That loved me, and alone; on shore, and when
Through scudding drifts the rainy Hyades
Vext the dim sea. I am become a name;
For always roaming with a hungry heart
Much have I seen and known: cities of men
And manners, climates, councils, governments,
Myself not least, but honored of them all,—
And drunk delight of battle with my peers,
Far on the ringing plains of windy Troy.
I am a part of all that I have met;
Yet all experience is an arch wherethrough
Gleams that untraveled world, whose margin fades
For ever and for ever when I move.
How dull it is to pause, to make an end,

To rust unburnished, not to shine in use!
As though to breathe were life. Life piled on life
Were all too little, and of one to me
Little remains: but every hour is saved
From that eternal silence, something more,
A bringer of new things; and vile it were
For some three suns to store and hoard myself,
And this gray spirit yearning in desire
To follow knowledge, like a sinking star,
Beyond the utmost bound of human thought.

    This is my son, mine own Telemachus,
To whom I leave the scepter and the isle—
Well-loved of me, discerning to fulfill
This labor, by slow prudence to make mild
A rugged people, and through soft degrees
Subdue them to the useful and the good.
Most blameless is he, centered in the sphere
Of common duties, decent not to fail
In offices of tenderness, and pay
Meet adoration to my household gods,
When I am gone. He works his work, I mine.

There lies the port: the vessel puffs her sail:
there gloom the dark broad seas. My mariners,
Souls that have toiled, and wrought, and thought
        with me—
That ever with a frolic welcome took
The thunder and the sunshine, and opposed
Free hearts, free foreheads—you and I are old;
Old age hath yet his honor and his toil;
Death closes all: but something ere the end,
Some work of noble note, may yet be done,
Not unbecoming men that strove with Gods.
The lights begin to twinkle from the rocks:
The long day wanes: the slow moon climbs: the deep
Moans round with many voices. Come, my friends,
'Tis not too late to seek a newer world.
Push off, and sitting well in order smite
The sounding furrows; for my purpose holds
To sail beyond the sunset, and the baths
Of all the western stars, until I die.
It may be that the gulfs will wash us down:
It may be we shall touch the Happy Isles,

And see the great Achilles, whom we knew.
Though much is taken, much abides; and though
We are not now that strength which in old days
Moved earth and heaven, that which we are, we
     are,—
One equal temper of heroic hearts,
Made weak by time and fate, but strong in will
To strive, to seek, to find, and not to yield.

ALFRED, LORD TENNYSON

Ode

We are the music-makers,
    And we are the dreamers of dreams,
Wandering by lone sea-breakers,
    And sitting by desolate streams;
World-losers and world-forsakers,
    On whom the pale moon gleams:
Yet we are the movers and shakers
    Of the world for ever, it seems.

With wonderful deathless ditties
We build up the world's cities,
    And out of a fabulous story
    We fashion an empire's glory:
One man with a dream, at pleasure,
    Shall go forth and conquer a crown;
And three with a new song's measure
    Can trample an empire down.

We, in the ages lying
    In the buried past of the earth,
Built Nineveh with our sighing,
    And Babel itself with our mirth;
And o'erthrew them with prophesying
    To the old of the new world's worth;
For each age is a dream that is dying,
    Or one that is coming to birth.

ARTHUR O'SHAUGHNESSY

Resignation

God grant me the serenity
To accept the things I cannot change;
The courage to change the things I can;
And the wisdom to know the difference.

REINHOLD NIEBUHR

Recessional

God of our fathers, known of old—
  Lord of our far-flung battle-line—
Beneath whose awful Hand we hold
  Dominion over palm and pine—
Lord God of Hosts, be with us yet,
Lest we forget, lest we forget!

The tumult and the shouting dies—
  The captains and the kings depart—
Still stands Thine ancient sacrifice,
  An humble and a contrite heart.
Lord God of Hosts, be with us yet,
Lest we forget, lest we forget!

Far-call'd our navies melt away—
  On dune and headland sinks the fire—
Lo, all our pomp of yesterday
  Is one with Nineveh and Tyre!
Judge of the Nations, spare us yet,
Let we forget, lest we forget!

If, drunk with sight of power, we loose
    Wild tongues that have not Thee in awe—
Such boasting as the Gentiles use
    Or lesser breeds without the Law—
Lord God of Hosts, be with us yet,
Lest we forget, lest we forget!

For heathen heart that puts her trust
    In reeking tube and iron shard—
All valiant dust that builds on dust,
    And guarding calls not Thee to guard—
For frantic boast and foolish word,
Thy Mercy on Thy People, Lord!

RUDYARD KIPLING

Prayer

God, though this life is but a wraith,
Although we know not what we use,
Although we grope with little faith,
Give me the heart to fight—and lose.

Ever insurgent let me be,
Make me more daring than devout;
From sleek contentment keep me free,
And fill me with a buoyant doubt.

Open my eyes to visions girt
With beauty, and with wonder lit—
But let me always see the dirt,
And all that spawn and die in it.

Open my ears to music; let
Me thrill with Spring's first flutes and drums—
But never let me dare forget
The bitter ballads of the slums.

From compromise and things half-done,
Keep me, with stern and stubborn pride.
And when, at last, the fight is won,
God, keep me still unsatisfied.

LOUIS UNTERMEYER

2 | 29

My Evening Prayer

If I have wounded any soul to-day,
If I have caused one foot to go astray,
If I have walked in my own wilful way—
    Good Lord, forgive!

If I have uttered idle words or vain,
If I have turned aside from want or pain,
Lest I myself should suffer through the strain—
    Good Lord, forgive!

If I have craved for joys that are not mine,
If I have let my wayward heart repine,
Dwelling on things of earth, not things divine—
    Good Lord, forgive!

If I have been perverse, or hard, or cold,
If I have longed for shelter in Thy fold,
When Thou hast given me some part to hold—
    Good Lord, forgive.

Forgive the sins I have confessed to Thee,
Forgive the secret sins I do not see,
That which I know not, Father, teach Thou me—
    Help me to live.

CHARLES H. GABRIEL

A Prayer

Let me do my work each day;
And if the darkened hours of despair overcome me,
May I not forget the strength that comforted me
In the desolation of other times.
May I still remember the bright hours that found me
Walking over the silent hills of my childhood,
Or dreaming on the margin of the quiet river,
When a light glowed within me,
And I promised my early God to have courage
Amid the tempests of the changing years.
Spare me from bitterness
And from the sharp passions of unguarded moments.
May I not forget that poverty and riches are of the
        spirit.
Though the world know me not,
May my thoughts and actions be such
As shall keep me friendly with myself.
Lift my eyes from the earth,
And let me not forget the uses of the stars.

Forbid that I should judge others,
Lest I condemn myself.
Let me not follow the clamor of the world,
But walk calmly in my path.
Give me a few friends who will love me for what I
am;
And keep ever burning before my vagrant steps
The kindly light of hope.
And though age and infirmity overtake me,
And I come not within sight of the castle of my
dreams,
Teach me still to be thankful for life,
And for time's olden memories that are good and
sweet;
And may the evening's twilight find me gentle still.

MAX EHRMANN

REFLECTIONS

A Wise Old Owl

A wise old owl lived in an oak;
The more he saw the less he spoke;
The less he spoke the more he heard:
Why can't we all be like that bird?

UNKNOWN

To a Fat Lady Seen From the Train

O why do you walk through the fields in gloves,
    Missing so much and so much?
O fat white woman, whom nobody loves,
Why do you walk through the fields in gloves,
When the grass is soft as the breast of doves
    And shivering-sweet to the touch?
O why do you walk through the fields in gloves,
    Missing so much and so much?

FRANCES CORNFORD

Get a Transfer

If you are on the Gloomy Line,
    Get a transfer.
If you're inclined to fret and pine,
    Get a transfer.
Get off the track of doubt and gloom,
Get on the Sunshine Track—there's room—
    Get a transfer.

If you're on the Worry Train,
    Get a transfer.
You must not stay there and complain,
    Get a transfer.
The Cheerful Cars are passing through,
And there's lots of room for you—
    Get a transfer.

If you're on the Grouchy Track,
    Get a transfer.
Just take a Happy Special back,
    Get a transfer.
Jump on the train and pull the rope,
That lands you at the station Hope—
    Get a transfer.

UNKNOWN

At Set of Sun

If you sit down at set of sun
And count the acts that you have done,
     And, counting, find
One self-denying deed, one word
That eased the heart of him who heard—
     One glance most kind,
That fell like sunshine where it went—
Then you may count that day well spent.

But, if, through all the livelong day,
You've cheered no heart, by yea or nay—
     If, through it all
You've nothing done that you can trace
That brought the sunshine to one face—
     No act most small
That helped some soul and nothing cost—
Then count that day as worse than lost.

GEORGE ELIOT

Grass

Pile the bodies high at Austerlitz and Waterloo.
Shovel them under and let me work—
    I am the grass; I cover all.

And pile them high at Gettysburg
And pile them high at Ypres and Verdun.
Shovel them under and let me work.
Two years, ten years, and passengers ask the
    conductor:
  What place is this?
  Where are we now?

  I am the grass.
  Let me work.

CARL SANDBURG

Who Hath a Book

Who hath a book
　　Has friends at hand,
And gold and gear
　　At his command;

And rich estates,
　　If he but look,
Are held by him
　　Who hath a book.

Who hath a book
　　Has but to read
And he may be
　　A king indeed;

His Kingdom is
　　His inglenook;
All this is his
　　Who hath a book.

WILBUR D. NESBIT

From Elegy Written in a Country Church-Yard

The curfew tolls the knell of parting day,
The lowing herd wind slowly o'er the lea,
The ploughman homeward plods his weary way,
And leaves the world to darkness, and to me.

The boast of heraldry, the pomp of power,
And all that beauty, all that wealth e'er gave
Awaits alike th' inevitable hour:—
The paths of glory lead but to the grave.

Full many a gem of purest ray serene
The dark unfathom'd caves of ocean bear:
Full many a flower is born to blush unseen,
And waste is sweetness on the desert air.

THOMAS GRAY

REMEMBRANCE

With Rue My Heart Is Laden

With rue my heart is laden
    For golden friends I had,
For many a rose-lipt maiden
    And many a lightfoot lad.

By brooks too broad for leaping
    The lightfoot boys are laid;
The rose-lipt girls are sleeping
    In fields where roses fade.

A.E. HOUSMAN

John Anderson, My Jo

John Anderson, my jo, John,
  When we were first acquent;
Your locks were like the raven,
  Your bonnie brow was brent;[1]
But now your brow is bald, John,
  Your locks are like the snow;
But blessings on your frosty pow,[2]
  John Anderson, my jo.

John Anderson, my jo, John,
  We clamb the hill thegither;
And mony a cantie[3] day, John,
  We've had wi' ane anither:
Now we maun totter down, John,
  And hand in hand we'll go,
And sleep thegither at the foot,
  John Anderson, my jo.

ROBERT BURNS

1. *bright*
2. *head*
3. *merry*

Daisy

Where the thistle lifts a purple crown
    Six foot out of the turf,
And the harebell shakes on the windy hill—
    O the breath of the distant surf!—

The hills look over on the South,
    And southward dreams the sea;
And, with the sea-breeze hand in hand,
    Came innocence and she.

Where 'mid the gorse the raspberry
    Red for the gatherer springs,
Two children did we stray and talk
    Wise, idle, childish things.

She listen'd with big-lipp'd surprise,
    Breast-deep 'mid flower and spine:
Her skin was like a grape, whose veins
    Run snow instead of wine.

She knew not those sweet words she spake,
    Nor knew her own sweet way;
But there's never a bird, so sweet a song
    Throng'd in whose throat that day!

O, there were flowers in Storrington
    On the turf and on the spray;
But the sweetest flower on Sussex hills
    Was the Daisy-flower that day!

Her beauty smooth'd earth's furrow'd face!
    She gave me tokens three:—
A look, a word of her winsome mouth,
    And a wild raspberry.

A berry red, a guileless look,
    A still word,—strings of sand!
And yet they made my wild, wild heart
    Fly down to her little hand.

For, standing artless as the air,
    And candid as the skies,
She took the berries with her hand,
    And the love with her sweet eyes.

The fairest things have fleetest end:
    Their scent survives their close,
But the rose's scent is bitterness
    To him that loved the rose!

She looked a little wistfully,
    Then went her sunshine way:—
The sea's eye had a mist on it,
    And the leaves fell from the day.

She went her unremembering way,
    She went, and left in me
The pang of all the partings gone,
    And partings yet to be.

She left me marvelling why my soul
    Was sad that she was glad;
At all the sadness in the sweet,
    The sweetness in the sad.

Still, still I seem'd to see her, still
    Look up with soft replies,
And take the berries with her hand,
    And the love with her lovely eyes.

Nothing begins, and nothing ends,
    That is not paid with moan;
For we are born in other's pain,
    And perish in our own.

FRANCIS THOMPSON

Ben Bolt

Don't you remember sweet Alice, Ben Bolt,—
 Sweet Alice whose hair was so brown,
Who wept with delight when you gave her a smile,
 And trembled with fear at your frown?
In the old churchyard in the valley, Ben Bolt,
 In a corner obscure and alone,
They have fitted a slab of the granite so gray,
 And Alice lies under the stone.

And don't you remember the school, Ben Bolt,
 With the master so cruel and grim,
And the shaded nook in the running brook
 Where the children went to swim?
Grass grows on the master's grave, Ben Bolt,
 The spring of the brook is dry,
And of all the boys who were schoolmates then
 There are only you and I.

THOMAS DUNN ENGLISH

I Remember, I Remember

I remember, I remember,
    The house where I was born,
The little window where the sun
    Came peeping in at morn:
He never came a wink too soon,
    Nor brought too long a day;
But now, I often wish the night
    Had borne my breath away.

I remember, I remember,
    The roses, red and white;
The violets and the lily-cups,
    Those flowers made of light!
The lilacs where the robin built,
    And where my brother set
The laburnum on his birthday,—
    The tree is living yet!

I remember, I remember,
    Where I was used to swing;
And thought the air must rush as fresh
    To swallows on the wing:
My spirit flew in feathers then,
    That is so heavy now,
And summer pools could hardly cool
    The fever on my brow!

I remember, I remember,
    The fir trees dark and high;
I used to think their slender tops
    Were close against the sky:
It was a childish ignorance,
    But now 'tis little joy
To know I'm farther off from heaven
    Than when I was a boy.

THOMAS HOOD

REVERENCE FOR LIFE

Woodman, Spare that Tree

Woodman, spare that tree!
 Touch not a single bough!
In youth it sheltered me,
 And I'll protect it now.
'Twas my forefather's hand
 That placed it near his cot;
There, woodman, let it stand,
 Thy axe shall harm it not!

That old familiar tree,
 Whose glory and renown
Are spread o'er land and sea,
 And wouldst thou hew it down?
Woodman, forbear thy stroke!
 Cut not its earth-bound ties;
O, spare that aged oak,
 Now towering to the skies!

When but an idle boy
   I sought its grateful shade;
In all their gushing joy
   Here too my sisters played.
My mother kissed me here;
   My father pressed my hand—
Forgive this foolish tear,
   But let that old oak stand!

My heart-strings round thee cling,
   Close as thy bark, old friend!
Here shall the wild-bird sing,
   And still thy branches bend.
Old tree! the storm still brave!
   And, woodman, leave the spot;
While I've a hand to save,
   Thy axe shall hurt it not.

GEORGE PERKINS MORRIS

Auguries of Innocence

To see a world in a grain of sand
And a Heaven in a wild flower,
Hold Infinity in the palm of your hand
And Eternity in an hour.

A robin redbreast in a cage
Puts all Heaven in a rage.
A dove-house filled with doves and pigeons
Shudders Hell through all its regions.
A dog starved at his master's gate
Predicts the ruin of the state.
A horse misused upon the road
Calls to Heaven for human blood.

Each outcry of the hunted hare
A fibre from the brain does tear.
A skylark wounded in the wing,
A cherubim does cease to sing.
The game cock clipped and armed for fight
Does the rising sun affright.
Every wolf's and lion's howl
Raises from Hell a human soul.

The wild deer wandering here and there
Keeps the human soul from care.
The lamb misused breeds public strife
And yet forgives the butcher's knife.
The bat that flits at close of eve
Has left the brain that won't believe.
The owl that calls upon the night
Speaks the unbeliever's fright.

He who shall hurt the little wren
Shall never be beloved by men.
He who the ox to wrath had moved
Shall never be by woman loved.

The wanton boy that kills the fly
Shall feel the spider's enmity.
He who torments the chafer's sprite
Weaves a bower in endless night.

The caterpillar on the leaf
Repeats to thee thy mother's grief.
Kill not the moth nor butterfly
For the Last Judgment draweth nigh.

WILLIAM BLAKE

The Fly

Little Fly,
Thy summer's play
My thoughtless hand
Has brushed away.

Am not I
A fly like thee?
Or art not thou
A man like me?

For I dance
And drink and sing,
Till some blind hand
Shall brush my wing.

If thought is life
And strength and breath,
And the want
Of thought is death,

Then am I
A happy fly
If I live
Or if I die.

WILLIAM BLAKE

ROMANCE

Delight in Disorder

A sweet disorder in the dress
Kindles in clothes a wantonness:
A lawn about the shoulders thrown
Into a fine distraction,
An erring lace, which here and there
Enthralls the crimson stomacher,
A cuff neglectful, and thereby
Ribbands to flow confusedly,
A winning wave (deserving note)
In the tempestuous petticoat,
A careless shoe-string, in whose tie
I see a wild civility,
Do more bewitch me, than when art
Is too precise in every part.

ROBERT HERRICK

What Care I

Shall I, wasting in despair,
Die because a woman's fair?
Or my cheeks make pale with care
'Cause another's rosy are?
Be she fairer than the day
Or the flowery meads in May—
 If she be not so to me,
 What care I how fair she be?

Great or good, or kind or fair,
I will ne'er the more despair;
If she love me, this believe,
I will die ere she shall grieve;

If she slight me when I woo,
I can scorn and let her go.
 For if she be not for me,
 What care I for whom she be?

GEORGE WITHER

Why So Pale and Wan

Why so pale and wan, fond lover?
   Prithee, why so pale?
Will, when looking well can't move her,
   Looking ill prevail?
   Prithee, why so pale?

Why so dull and mute, young sinner?
   Prithee, why so mute?
Will, when speaking well can't win her,
   Saying nothing do 't?
   Prithee, why so mute?

Quit, quit for shame! This will not move;
   This cannot take her.
If of herself she will not love,
   Nothing can make her.
   The devil take her!

SIR JOHN SUCKLING

What My Lover Said

By the merest chance, in the twilight gloom,
    In the orchard path he met me;
In the tall, wet grass, with its faint perfume,
And I tried to pass, but he made no room,
    Oh, I tried, but he would not let me.
So I stood and blushed till the grass grew red,
    With my face bent down above it,
While he took my hand as he whispering said—
(How the clover lifted each pink, sweet head,
To listen to all that my lover said;
    Oh, the clover in bloom, I love it!)

In the high, wet grass went the path to hide,
    And the low, wet leaves hung over;
But I could not pass upon either side,
For I found myself, when I vainly tried,
    In the arms of my steadfast lover.
And he held me there and he raised my head,
    While he closed the path before me,
And he looked down into my eyes and said—
(How the leaves bent down from the boughs
      o'er head,
To listen to all that my lover said;
    Oh, the leaves hanging lowly o'er me!)

Had he moved aside but a litle way,
    I could surely then have passed him;
And he knew I never could wish to stay,
And would not have heard what he had to say,
    Could I only aside have cast him.
It was almost dark, and the moments sped,
    And the searching night wind found us,
But he drew me nearer and softly said—
(How the pure, sweet wind grew still, instead,
To listen to all that my lover said;
    Oh, the whispering wind around us!)

I know that the grass and the leaves will not tell,
    And I'm sure that the wind, precious rover,
Will carry my secret so safely and well
    That no being shall ever discover

One word of the many that rapidly fell
    From the soul-speaking lips of my lover;
    And from the moon and the stars that looked over
Shall never reveal what a fairy-like spell
They wove round about us that night in the dell,
    In the path through the dew-laden clover,
Nor echo the whispers that made my heart swell
    As they fell from the lips of my lover.

HOMER GREENE

The Highwayman

Part One

The wind was a torrent of darkness among the gusty
      trees,
The moon was a ghostly galleon tossed upon cloudy
      seas,
The road was a ribbon of moonlight over the purple
      moor,
And the highwayman came riding—
    Riding—riding—
The highwayman came riding, up to the old inn-door.

He'd a French cocked-hat on his forehead, a bunch of
      lace at his chin,
A coat of claret velvet, and breeches of brown
      doeskin:
They fitted with never a wrinkle; his boots were up to
      the thigh!
And he rode with a jewelled twinkle,
    His pistol butts a-twinkle,
His rapier hilt a-twinkle, under the jewelled sky.

Over the cobbles he clattered and clashed in the dark
      inn-yard,
And he tapped with his whip on the shutters, but all
      was locked and barred:
He whistled a tune to the window, and who should be
      waiting there
But the landlord's black-eyed daughter,
   Bess, the landlord's daughter,
Plaiting a dark red love-knot into her long black hair.

And then in the dark old inn-yard a stable-wicket
      creaked
Where Tim, the ostler, listened; his face was white
      and peaked,
His eyes were hollows of madness, his hair like moldy
      hay;
But he loved the landlord's daughter,
   The landlord's red-lipped daughter:
Dumb as a dog he listened, and he heard the robber
      say—

"One kiss, my bonny sweetheart, I'm after a prize
      tonight,
But I shall be back with the yellow gold before the
      morning light.
Yet if they press me sharply, and harry me through
      the day,

Then look for me by moonlight,

    Watch for me by moonlight:

I'll come to thee by moonlight, though Hell should
      bar the way."

He rose upright in the stirrups, he scarce could reach
      her hand;

But she loosened her hair i' the casement! His face
      burnt like a brand

As the black cascade of perfume came tumbling over
      his breast;

And he kissed its waves in the moonlight,

    (Oh, sweet black waves in the moonlight)

Then he tugged at his reins in the moonlight, and
      galloped away to the West.

Part Two

He did not come in the dawning; he did not come at
      noon;

And out of the tawny sunset, before the rise o' the
      moon,

When the road was a gypsy's ribbon, looping the pur-
      ple moor,

A red-coat-troop came marching—

    Marching—marching—

King George's men came marching, up to the old inn-
      door.

They said no word to the landlord, they drank his ale
    instead;
But they gagged his daughter and bound her to the
    foot of her narrow bed.
Two of them knelt at her casement, with muskets at
    the side!
There was death at every window;
    And Hell at one dark window;
For Bess could see, through her casement, the road
    that *he* would ride.

They had tied her up to attention, with many a snig-
    gering jest:
They had bound a musket beside her, with the barrel
    beneath her breast!
"Now keep good watch!" and they kissed her.
    She heard the dead man say—
Look for me by moonlight;
    Watch for me by moonlight;
I'll come to thee by moonlight, though Hell should
    bar the way!

She twisted her hands behind her; but all the knots
    held good!
She writhed her hands till her fingers were wet with
    sweat or blood!
They stretched and strained in the darkness, and the
    hours crawled by like years;

Till, now, on the stroke of midnight,
   Cold, on the stroke of midnight,
The tip of one finger touched it! The trigger at least
      was hers!

The tip of one finger touched it; she strove no more
      for the rest!
Up, she stood up to attention, with the barrel beneath
      her breast,
She would not risk their hearing: she would not strive
      again;
For the road lay bare in the moonlight,
   Blank and bare in the moonlight;
And the blood of her veins in the moonlight throbbed
      to her Love's refrain.

Tlot-tlot, tlot-tlot! Had they heard it? The horse-hoofs
      ringing clear—
Tlot-tlot, tlot-tlot, in the distance? Were they deaf
      that they did not hear?
Down the ribbon of moonlight, over the brow of the
      hill,
The highwayman came riding,
   Riding, riding!
The red-coats looked to their priming! She stood up
      straight and still!

Tlot-tlot, in the frosty silence; *Tlot-tlot* in the echoing
    night!
Nearer he came and nearer! Her face was like a light!
Her eyes grew wide for a moment; she drew one last
    deep breath,
Then her finger moved in the moonlight,
    Her musket shattered the moonlight,
Shattered her breast in the moonlight and warned
    him—with her death.

He turned; he spurred him Westward; he did not
    know who stood
Bowed with her head o'er the musket, drenched with
    her own red blood!
Not till the dawn he heard it, and slowly blanched to
    hear
How Bess, the landlord's daughter,
    The landlord's black-eyed daughter,
Had watched for her Love in the moonlight; and died
    in the darkness there.

Back, he spurred like a madman, shrieking a curse to
    the sky,
With the white road smoking behind him, and his
    rapier brandished high!
Blood-red were his spurs i' the golden noon; wine-red
    was his velvet coat;

When they shot him down on the highway,
  Down like a dog on the highway,
And he lay in his blood on the highway, with the
  bunch of lace at his throat.

And still a winter's night, they say, when the wind is
  in the trees,
When the moon is a ghostly galleon tossed upon
  cloudy seas,
When the road is a ribbon of moonlight over the pur-
  ple moor,
A highwayman comes riding—
  Riding—riding—
A highwayman comes riding, up to the old inn-door.

Over the cobbles he clatters and clangs in the dark
  inn-yard;
And he taps with his whip on the shutters, but all is
  locked and barred:
He whistles a tune to the window, and who should be
  waiting there
But the landlord's black-eyed daughter,
  Bess, the landlord's daughter,
Plaiting a dark red love-knot into her long black hair.

ALFRED NOYES

If We Knew

If we knew the woe and heartache
    Waiting for us down the road,
If our lips could taste the wormwood,
    If our backs could feel the load,
Would we waste the day in wishing
    For a time that ne'er can be?
Would we wait in such impatience
    For our ships to come from sea?

If we knew the baby fingers
    Pressed against the windowpane

Would be cold and stiff tomorrow—
    Never trouble us again—
Would the bright eyes of our darling
    Catch the frown upon our brow?
Would the print of rosy fingers
    Vex us then as they do now?

Ah! these little ice-cold fingers—
    How they point our memories back
To the hasty words and actions
    Strewn along our backward track!
How these little hands remind us,
    As in snowy grace they lie,
Not to scatter thorns—but roses—
    For our reaping by and by.

Strange we never prize the music
    Till the sweet-voiced bird has flown;
Strange that we should slight the violets
    Till the lovely flowers are gone;
Strange that summer skies and sunshine
    Never seem one half so fair
As when winter's snowy pinions
    Shake their white down in the air!

Lips from which the seal of silence
    None but God can roll away,
Never blossomed in such beauty
    As adorns the mouth today;
And sweet words that freight our memory
    With their beautiful perfume,
Come to us in sweeter accents
    Through the portals of the tomb.

Let us gather up the sunbeams
    Lying all around our path;
Let us keep the wheat and roses,
    Casting out the thorns and chaff;
Let us find our sweetest comfort
    In the blessings of today,
With a patient hand removing
    All the briars from the way.

MAY RILEY SMITH

Tell Her So

Amid the cares of married strife
    In spite of toil and business life
If you value your dear wife—
    Tell her so!

When days are dark and deeply blue
    She has her troubles, same as you
Show her that your love is true
    Tell her so!

Whether you mean or care,
Gentleness, kindness, love, and hate,
Envy, anger, are there.
Then, would you quarrels avoid
And peace and love rejoice?
Keep anger not only out of your words—
Keep it out of your voice.

AUTHOR UNKNOWN

INDEX OF FIRST LINES

INDEX OF AUTHORS

ACKNOWLEDGMENTS

Thanks to the following publishers for their permission to reprint the poems listed:

ANTHEM FOR DOOMED YOUTH from *Collected Poems of Wilfred Owen*. Copyright Chatto & Windus Ltd. 1963. Reprinted by permission of New Directions Publishing Corporation.

CARRY ON from *The Collected Poems of Robert Service*. Reprinted by permission of Dodd, Mead & Company, Inc. Copyright renewed 1944 by Robert W. Service. Thanks to McGraw-Hill Ryerson Limited of Scarborough, Ontario, Canada, for permission to reprint this poem in Canada.

COOL TOMBS, and GRASS from *Cornhuskers* by Carl Sandburg, copyright 1918 by Holt, Rinehart and Winston, Inc.; copyright 1946 by Carl Sandburg. Reprinted by permission of Harcourt Brace Jovanovich, Inc.

DEATH IS A DOOR by Nancy Byrd Turner. Reprinted by permission of The Golden Quill Press.

FLEURETTE from *The Collected Poems of Robert Service*. Copyright 1916 by Dodd, Mead & Company. Copyright renewed 1944 by Robert W. Service. Thanks to McGraw-Hill Ryerson Limited of Scarborough, Ontario, Canada, for permission to reprint this poem in Canada.

I SHALL NOT CARE from *Collected Poems of Sara Teasdale*. Reprinted with permission of Macmillan Publishing Co., Inc. Copyright 1915 by Macmillan Publishing Co., Inc., renewed 1943 by Mamie T. Whiless.

A HART BOOK

A & W PUBLISHERS
New York